ENGINEER DEPARTMENT, UNITED STATES ARMY.

REPORT

ON THE

COMPRESSIVE STRENGTH, SPECIFIC GRAVITY,

AND

RATIO OF ABSORPTION

OF

VARIOUS KINDS OF BUILDING-STONE FROM DIFFERENT SECTIONS OF THE UNITED STATES,

TESTED AT

FORT TOMPKINS, STATEN ISLAND, N. Y.

BY

Q. A. GILLMORE,

LIEUT. COL. CORPS OF ENGINEERS, BVT. MAJ. GEN. U. S. A.

WASHINGTON:
GOVERNMENT PRINTING OFFICE.
1874.

ENGINEER OFFICE, *New York, July* 30, 1874.

GENERAL: I have the honor to submit herewith a report on the *compressive strength*, *specific gravity*, and *ratio* of *absorption* of various kinds of building-stone from different sections of the United States, tested by me in person, or under my directions, at Fort Tompkins, Staten Island, within the last eighteen months.

A sheet of drawings accompanies this report, showing the hydrostatic press used for crushing the specimens, and several somewhat peculiar forms of breakage.

Very respectfully, your obedient servant,

Q. A. GILLMORE,
Lt. Col. of Engineers, Bvt. Maj. Gen. U. S. A.

Brig. Gen. A. A. HUMPHREYS,
Chief of Engineers, U. S. A.

NOTE.—In making the tests, and preparing this report, valuable assistance was rendered by Capt. D. P. Heap, Corps of Engineers, and by Messrs. Louis Nickerson, John L. Suess, and James Cocroft.

Q. A. G.

[Indorsement.]

OFFICE OF THE CHIEF OF ENGINEERS,
Washington, D. C., August 10, 1874.

Respectfully submitted to the honorable Secretary of War. This paper contains valuable information for the officers of the Corps of Engineers, and I respectfully recommend that authority may be granted to have it printed at the Public Printer's; the plates to be prepared in this office.

A. A. HUMPHREYS,
Brig. Gen. and Chief of Engineers.

Approved by the Secretary of War August 12, 1874.

REPORT.

OBJECTS USED FOR TESTING.

The majority of stones experimented upon were delivered from the quarries in the form of true cubes, measuring two inches each way; while some had to be cut to that shape at Fort Tompkins. Generally speaking, the stones were quite true and regular in shape. To distribute the pressure more evenly over the whole surface of the stone, each cube was placed between two cushions of soft pine-wood, measuring $2'' \times 2'' \times \frac{3}{8}''$; one of them on top of the cube, and the other at its bottom.

This arrangement also caused the pressure to act more gradually. The wooden cushions, becoming much indented by the effects of the pressure, to some extent took the place of mortar, which would be used in actual building.

For iron and wood, Hodgkinson has shown that trial-specimens should be at least $1\frac{1}{2}$ times as high as the width of bed; but as stone, except when used in columns, is always made of less height than bed, the cubical form of specimens adopted for the experiments affords sufficient security against angular breakage.

APPARATUS FOR TESTING.

The apparatus employed for testing is a hydrostatic press, known as the Hoe press, and shown in Figs. 1 and 2 of the diagram accompanying this report. The pump, *b*, stands on a tank, *a*, filled with water, with a suction-pipe running nearly to its bottom. The plunger, *c*, is worked by a hand-lever, *g*, attached to a cross-head, *h*, and guided by the rod, *d*, passing through the guide, *e*, which forms part of the standard, *f*. The power, or purchase, of the hand-lever can be adjusted by changing its fulcrum to either one of the three pin-holes of the standard.

A connecting-pipe, *k*, leads from the pump to the lower end of the cylinder, *m*, of the press. When the pump is worked, the water is forced through this pipe into the cylinder, and gradually lifts the piston, or ram, *n*, which in this case had a diameter of $4\frac{1}{2}$ inches. A leather disk is fixed to the lower end of the ram, which becomes expanded by the pressure of the fluid, and makes the ram water-tight. The table, or beam, *o*, is lifted up together with the ram, as well as the movable piece, *p*, which had to be used in these experiments merely on account of the small size of the samples tested.

The stone to be tested is placed on top of *p*, between two pieces of pine wood, as already mentioned, and gradually raised until it touches the lower face of the beam, or cross-head, *q*. By continued pumping, the pressure is increased until the stone crushes, and the amount of pressure noted by means of the gauges. The upper beam, *q*, is connected to the bottom beam by four wrought-iron rods, *r*, 1¾ inches thick, which, it will be seen, are subjected to a tensile strain only, after the pressure exceeds the weight of the upper cross-beam. All the other parts of the press are of cast iron.

GAUGES.

The press is supplied with two gauges, one indicating the pressure up to 100,000 pounds; the other to only 5,000 pounds, as shown in Fig. 1. Both are connected by pipes with the lower end of the cylinder of the ram. Both gauges may be used simultaneously until the capacity of the 5,000-pound gauge is exhausted, when its connection with the cylinder is shut off by a little valve worked by a hand-wheel. Generally, in testing stones, the lighter gauge is not used.

To check the working of the 100,000-pound gauge next to the press, another gauge of similar capacity was employed as a test-gauge. It is attached to the connecting-pipe, *k*, near to the pump. These gauges were manufactured in the city of New York on a modified arrangement of Bourdon's principle.

The 100,000-pound gauge attached to the press is shown in Figs. 3, 4, and 5, drawn half-size. This gauge, like the two others, has a dial-face, traversed by two hands of unequal length. One of these is moved directly by the power of the press; the other (shorter) hand is simply carried along by means of a little projecting pin on the back of the longer hand, or power-needle. The latter returns to the zero-point as soon as the pressure ceases, leaving the shorter hand at the maximum point reached on the scale. The record can thus easily be read off, after which the record-needle is pushed back to the zero-point in readiness for another trial.

The mechanism of the gauge consists essentially of the following parts: A curved steel tube, (3), communicates at one end, by means of the pipe (1), with the cylinder of the hydrostatic ram; but it is closed at the other end. The cross-section of this tube is flattened or elliptical; its greater breadth being perpendicular to the plane in which the tube is curved. When power is applied, the water entering the tube tends to straighten it out, causing it to become less curved in proportion to the power used. This is explained by the fact that the area of the outer side of the bent tube is larger than the area of the inner side; the surplus of pressure on the outside tends to straighten the tube.

The closed end of the tube communicates its motion by means of the link (4) to a lever, (6), pivoted between two little standards (5), which are screwed to the block (2). The lever (6) is made of the shape of an open rectangular frame; its two pivots being nearer one of its ends than the other. Within this lever-frame another smaller frame is fitted, having in its center a pin to which the link (4) is hung. By means of two little set-screws, one at each end of the lever-frame, the link-frame can be adjusted to the proper distance from the pivots of the lever-frame.

The lever-frame (6) has a toothed segment, (7), attached to it, which gears into a small pinion, (8,) fixed on the spindle of the power-needle. A delicate spiral spring, (9), is fixed with its central end to that spindle, while its circumferential end is held in a stud of one of the standards (5) between the spindle and the fulcrum of the lever. When power is applied, the bent tube gradually changes its form to a more straightened curve; the link moves the lever, which, in its turn, by its toothed segment, turns the little pinion, and consequently also the power-needle fixed to the spindle of the pinion. As soon as the pressure ceases, the bent tube assumes its previous form, and the hand, or needle, returns to zero, aided by the reaction of the unwinding spiral spring.

The graduations on the dial-plate of the gauge are fixed by comparison with an air-manometer, or with another Bourdon gauge, known to be correctly graduated; and the correctness of the gauge is guaranteed by the manufacturer. But it is, of course, desirable to be otherwise well assured of the accuracy of the records obtained. For the series of experiments herein spoken of, a check was obtained, as already mentioned, by means of another 100,000-pound gauge near the pump, so that, a test between these two gauges once established, either one can be taken off when rough work is to be done, (the most sensitive one always,) and the other used, and then both tested again. By this means there can be no change that would escape the notice of an attentive operator, and the actual power used can at any time be tested in full by the application of either gauge to a hydraulic press having a lever-accompaniment.

WEIGHT OF MOVABLE PART OF RAM AND FRICTION.

The weight of the movable part of the press is nearly 780 pounds, which, with its own friction, amounts to 800 pounds nearly. This is to be subtracted from the "strength of specimen," or 200 pounds from the strength per square inch. Much dispute has existed about the friction of the hydrostatic press when performing heavy duty. Rankine made some rough experiments, which caused him to estimate the friction at 10 per cent. I. Hicks, civil engineer, of Bolton, England, found, by very careful and long-continued trials made regardless of expense, that the friction varies with the diameter of the ram, and that it is very small and very certain. By his trials the friction of the ram used in the experiments herein discussed (the cylinder being of $4\frac{1}{2}$ inches diameter) would amount to $\frac{9}{10}$ per cent. only, or say 1 per cent. This could and should be tested upon the individual ram; but, without special and costly appliances, it will have to be got at indirectly, and, therefore, slowly.

PRELIMINARY REMARKS.

The diagram accompanying this report shows sketches of ten samples of stone. The first one, named homogeneous stone, is imaginary, and represents the general form of breakage of many sandstones and saccharine marbles. The separate pieces shown are such as are usually picked up after breakage, although with other varieties of stone they are generally more angular. The other nine sketches of stone represent samples actually tested and broken. The numbers given with each of them correspond with those in the tables. The position of the cube when tested is also stated, whether it was placed on "bed" or on "edge."

THE BREAKAGE OF STONE.

Considering the infinitely-varied composition and character of all kinds of rock, it may be said that no material is less calculated to permit the establishment of special laws by a general form of breakage. It may be safely assumed, however, that more numerous and extended experiments, carefully and patiently conducted, will ultimately lead to the development of certain general laws relating to the behavior of stones under pressure, a knowledge of which will be most useful to the engineer and builder.

Homogeneous stones seem, in most cases, to break in the following manner, (see diagram:) The forms of fragments *a* and *b* are approximately either conical or pyramidal, according as the stone is friable and of obviously granular structure, like sandstone and a few kinds of marble and granite, or compact, such as the true limestones and most marbles and granites. The more or less disk-shaped pieces *c* and *d* are detached from the sides of the cube with a sort of explosion, flying off in a more or less intact condition. In *e* and *f*, the stone is generally found crushed and ground to powder by the attrition of the larger fragments. Of course, this general result, or law, is modified by the nature and quality of the "grain" in the stone, and those other causes of irregularity which leave no two cubes of the same strength and condition, although they may have been cut directly apart from each other.

This form of breakage occurs also in non-homogeneous stones broken "on bed;" but it must be remembered that here the modification must be taken into account which "grain" produces as against homogeneity, rendering the object liable to split in rectangular fragments. This frequently lengthens the cone or pyramid in stones "on bed," and causes those set "on edge" to actually split in rectangular disks; the style of splitting being, of course, irregularly modified for different specimens. Sand-cracks, &c., in stones, have also their influence in directing the pressure, and even the difficulty of determining the "bed" in some stones, after being cut, may be a source of errors.

The two strangest cases of abnormal breakage occurred in the United States Quarry limestone, (Nos. 29 and 30 of table,) the first of which, "on bed," threw off a couple of thin fragments, and then exploded; the balance of the stone being scattered about in minute particles. The second, "on edge," broke into wedge-shaped disks of moderate size.

The Du Luth, dark granite (Nos. 73 and 74) split "on bed" into two disks nearly equal in size, which were forced a half-inch apart, though pressed at right angles to their line of motion by a force of 68,000 pounds. The second specimen, "on edge," acted in precisely the same manner. A very curious result of this experiment was the fact that the pine cushion-blocks, which usually stand a pressure of 80,000 or 90,000 pounds, and become indented but comparatively not torn or injured, were in this case spread over the pieces *a* and *b* as though the wood had been crushed to fiber in liquid resin and painted over with a brush, part of it coming down in rough festoon between the separated parts of the stone.

But notwithstanding the diversity of phenomena attending the breakage of stones by direct compression, the obvious difference between the fragments produced by that operation and those fragments obtained by the stone-cutter's hammer is suggestive of laws, modified but always existing, and capable of being at least roughly classified.

SPECIFIC GRAVITY.

The stones whose resistance to crushing-pressure had been tested were also experimented upon in relation to their specific gravity. In the course of these investigations, it was sometimes necessary to be content with rather small fragments of stone, of not more than 15 to 18 penny-weight; but generally they weighed from one to two ounces.

On commencing this part of the work, some doubt was felt in regard to the best means of obtaining the correct displacement of porous stones; and all stones are more or less porous. It appeared evident that in weighing the stone first in air and then in water, an error would be committed by saturation. The first idea, to give the stone a coating of thin varnish was abandoned, because, although the pellicle would be thin, yet no means could be taken to know precisely what its thickness was, or what it amounted to in its effects. The second idea, to soak the stone in very fluid reisn, the pellicle to be washed from the surface before dry, was given up because it was desirable to preserve the specimens intact for experiments on freezing and other tests.

The plan finally adopted was, first, to remove from the stone all loose particles, and round off all sharp corners and edges, bringing it, in fact, practically to that condition commonly known as "water-worn." It was then carefully weighed in air, immersed in water, and allowed to remain there until all bubbling had ceased, and its weight taken. It was then taken out of the water, and weighed again, in its saturated condition, with the precaution of, previously denuding the stone of superabundant water by being compressed lightly in bibulous paper. The specific gravity is now found by dividing the weight of the stone when perfectly dry by its weight in the air after having been saturated *minus* its weight in water.

This may also be expressed by the formula—

$$\text{Specific gravity} = \frac{W}{W_{\prime\prime} - W_{\prime}}$$

W representing weight of dry stone in air; $W_{\prime}$ representing weight of saturated stone in air; $W_{\prime}$ representing weight of stone immersed in water.

In determining the specific gravity of stone, the weight of water was assumed to be 62½ pounds per cubic foot.

RATIO OF ABSORPTION.

The term "ratio of absorption" simply expresses the weight of water absorbed by the stone as compared with the weight of the dry stone; that is, if the stone when dry weighs 300 units, and the column of "ratio of absorption" shows the fraction $\frac{1}{300}$, it means that, by immersion in water, the stone will absorb 1 unit of it, weighing 301 units immediately after its removal from the water.

The method adopted for ascertaining the specific weight of stone furnished at the same time the means to determine the "ratio of absorption." The weight of the saturated stone minus the weight of the dry stone gives, as a result, the amount of water absorbed. This might, perhaps, more correctly be called the "avidity of absorption," since it was limited to the period of bubbling. Some few stones, having been kept immersed in water for several consecutive days, showed a slight increase in weight.

Since the capacity of a stone to absorb water has much influence on its durability even during the warm season, and far more so in cold weather, the addition to the tables of this column was deemed advisable.

Crushing-strength of granites in two-inch cubes.

Number.	Kind.	Locality.	Position.	Cracked.	Strength of specimen.	Strength per square inch.	Specific gravity.	Weight of one cubic foot.	Ratio of absorption.	Remarks.
				Pounds.	*Pounds.*	*Pounds.*		*Pounds.*		
1	Blue	Staten Island, N. Y	On bed	24, 000	89, 000	22, 250	2. 861	178. 8	Absorption too slow to be taken while weighing. (Nos. 1–34)	Cracked before bursting.
2		Fox Island, Me			59, 500	14, 875	2. 631	164. 1		Burst suddenly.
3		Dix Island, Me			60, 000	15, 000	2. 635	166. 5		Do.
4	Dark	Quincy, Mass		19, 500	71, 000	17, 750	2. 660	166. 2		Cracked before bursting.
5	Light	do		18, 000	59, 000	14, 750	2. 695	168. 7		Do.
6		Tarrytown, Westchester County, N. Y	On bed	22, 000	73, 000	18, 250	2. 655	162. 2		Do.
7	Flagging	North River, N. Y			53, 700	13, 425	2. 690	168. 1		Broke suddenly without cracking.
8	Old Quarry	Westerly, Washington County, R. I			71, 000	17, 750	2. 646	165. 6		Do.
9	do	do			69, 000	17, 250	2. 646	165. 6		Do.
10		Millstone Point, Conn			64, 750	16, 187	2. 706	168. 7		Do.
11		do			75, 000	18, 750	2. 706	168. 7		Do.
12		Sprucehead, Me			54, 000	13, 500	2. 750	171. 9		Do.
13		do			70, 000	17, 500	2. 750	171. 9		Do.
14		Hewitt's Island, Me			57, 500	14, 375	2. 634	164. 6		Do.
15		do			60, 250	15, 062	2. 634	164. 6		Do.
16	Up river	Richmond, Va			85, 000	21, 250				Do.
17	do	do			80, 000	20, 000				Do.
18		Greenwich, Conn			45, 200	11, 300	2. 835	177. 2		Do.
19		do			46, 800	11, 700	2. 835	177. 2		Do.
20	Niantic River	New London, Conn			50, 000	12, 500	2. 660	166. 25		Do.
21	do	do	On edge		56, 700	14, 175	2. 660	166. 25		Do.
22		Fox Island, Me	On bed		60, 250	15, 062	2. 660	166. 3		Do.
23		do			46, 800	11, 700	2. 660	166. 3		Do.
24		Vinalhaven, Me			52, 600	13, 150	2. 720	170. 0		Do.
25		do			67, 000	16, 750	2. 720	170. 0		Do.
26	Harlem stone	Morrisania, Westchester County, N. Y			63, 200	15, 800	2. 720	170. 0		Do.
27	Tombstone	Sharkey's Quarry, Me			88, 500	22, 125	2. 720	170. 0		Do.
28	do	do			83, 500	20, 875	2. 720	170. 0		Do.
29		Richmond, Va			64, 250	16, 063	2. 727	170. 5		Do.
30		Cape Ann, Mass	On bed		59, 750	12, 423				Do.
31		do	do		78, 000	19, 500				Do.
32	Porter's rock	Mystic River, Conn	do		72, 500	18, 125	2. 630	164. 4		Do.
33	do	do	On edge		89, 000	22, 250	2. 630	164. 4		Do.
34	Gray	Westerly, R. I	On bed		58, 750	14, 687	2. 670	166. 9		Do.
35	do	do	On edge		59, 750	14, 937	2. 670	166. 9	1-348	Do.
36	do	Richmond, Va	On bed		56, 400	14, 100	2. 630	164. 4	1-348	Do.
37	do	do	do		55, 500	13, 875	2. 630	164. 4	1-230	Do.
38	do	New Haven, Conn	On edge	29, 000	31, 000	7, 750	2. 600	162. 5	1-230	Waxy-looking, having a resinous luster.
39	do	do	On bed		38, 000	9, 500	2. 600	162. 5	1-230	Burst suddenly.
40	do	Stony Creek, Conn	do		60, 000	15, 000	2. 645	165. 4	1-201	Do.

Crushing-strength of granites in two-inch cubes—Continued.

Number.	Kind.	Locality.	Position.	Cracked.	Strength of specimen.	Strength per square inch.	Specific gravity.	Weight of one cubic foot.	Ratio of absorption.	Remarks.
				Pounds.	*Pounds.*	*Pounds.*		*Pounds.*		
41	Gray	Stony Creek, Conn	On edge		67,000	16,750	2.645	165.4	1-201	Burst suddenly.
42	do	do	On bed		63,000	15,750	2.645	165.4	1-201	Do.
43	do	Fall River, Mass	do		63,750	15,937	2.635	165.	1-216	Do.
44	do	do	On edge	33,000	37,000	9,250	2.635	165.	1-216	First split vertically.
45	Rose	Niantic, Conn	On bed		38,200	9,550	2.600	162.5	1-704	Burst suddenly; pores supposed filled with red pigment.
46	Gray	do	do		37,800	9,450	2.580	161.2	1-254	Burst suddenly.
47	Gneiss	Sachemshead Quarry, Conn	On edge		63,750	15,937	2.620	163.7	1-162	Do.
48	do	do	On bed		56,000	14,000	2.620	163.7	1-162	Do.
49	Gray	Hurricane Island, Me	do	33,000	57,700	14,425	2.670	166.9		
50	do	do	On edge		59,750	14,937	2.670	166.9		Burst suddenly.
51	do	do	On bed		44,000	11,000	2.670	166.9		Split off considerably before bursting.
52	Dark, soft-looking	Madison Avenue, N. Y	do		45,000	11,250	2.920	182.5	0	Probably contains an unusual quantity of iron.
53	do	do	On edge		50,000	12,500	2.920	182.5	0	
54	Gray	Port Deposit, Md	On bed		79,000	19,750	2.720	170.	0	Coarse; strongly dashed with black.
55	do	do	On edge	33,000	52,400	13,100	2.720	170.	0	Do.
56	do	do	On bed		66,000	16,500	2.720	170.	0	Do.
57	do	do	do		60,000	15,000	2.720	170.	0	Burst suddenly.
58	do	Garrison's, North River, N. Y	On edge	48,000	49,000	12,250	2.580	161.3	1-167	
59	do	do	On bed	51,000	53,500	13,370	2.580	161.3	1-167	
60	do	Palmer Quarry, Me	do	41,000	46,000	11,500	2.590	161.9	1-150	
61	do	do	On edge	58,000	66,000	16,500	2.590	161.9	1-150	
62	do	Rockport, Mass	On bed		65,200	16,300	2.610	163.2	1-152	
63	do	do	On edge	36,000	79,000	19,750	2.610	163.2	1-152	
64	Dark	Du Luth, Minn	On bed		71,000	17,750	2.780	173.7	1-711	Syenitic; or, perhaps, trap-rock.
65	do	do	do		76,000	19,000	2.800	175.	0	
66	do	do	do		67,300	16,825	2.800	175.	0	Scant.
67	Purplish	Huron Island, Mich	do		72,500	18,125	2.630	164.4	1-659	
68	Grayish-rose	do	do		82,600	20,650	2.66	166.2	1-600	
69	do	do	On edge		57,700	14,425	2.62	163.7	1-363	Soaked a week for absorption.
70	Grayish	Chaumont Bay, N. Y	On bed		91,000	22,750	2.65	165.	1-355	Do.
71	do	do	do		64,200	16,050	2.65	165.	1-350	Do.
72	do	do	do		70,000	17,500	2.66	166.2	1-557	
73	Dark	Du Luth, Minn	do		68,000	17,000	(*)	(*)	(*)	
74	do	do	On edge		68,750	17,187	(*)	(*)	(*)	
75	Light	Saint Cloud, Stearns County, Minn	On bed		64,000	16,000	2.69	168.2	1-239	
76	do	do	On edge		74,000	18,500	2.69	168.2	1-239	
77	Bluish-gray	Keene, Cheshire County, N. H	On bed		41,000	10,375	2.656	166.	1-300	Used in inside of new capitol, Albany, N. Y.
78	do	do	do		51,500	12,875	2.656	166.	1-300	

Crushing-strength of limestones in two-inch cubes.

1	Glen's Falls	Glen's Falls, Warren County, N. Y	On bed		45, 900	11, 475	2. 700	168. 8		All the stones named below burst without cracking, except those noted to the contrary.
2	...do	......do	On edge		43, 000	10, 750	2. 700	168. 8		
3	Lake	Lake Champlain, N. Y	On bed		100, 000	25, 000	2. 75	171. 9		
4	...do	......do	On edge	60, 000	86, 000	21, 500	2. 75	171. 9		
5		Canajoharie, Montgomery County, N. Y	On bed	70, 000	82, 800	20, 700	2. 685	169. 8		
6		......do	On edge	70, 000	77, 000	19, 250	2. 685	169. 8		
7	North River	Kingston, N. Y	On bed	40, 000	55, 600	13, 900	2. 69	168. 2		
8	...do	......do	On edge		44, 200	11, 050	2. 69	168. 2		
9		Garrison's Station, N. Y	On bed		74, 000	18, 500	2. 635	164. 7		
10		......do	On edge		73, 100	18, 275	2. 635	164. 7		
11		......do	On bed		71, 000	17, 750	2. 62	163. 7		
12		......do	....do		71, 000	17, 750	2. 616	163. 5		
13		......do	....do		75, 100	18, 775	2. 616	163. 5		
14	White	Marblehead, Ohio	....do		45, 000	11, 250	2. 4	150.	1-30	
15	...do	......do	....do		42. 800	10, 700	2. 4	150.	1-33	
16	...do	......do	....do		50, 400	12, 600	2. 48	155.	1-33	
17	...do	Joliet, Ill	....do		51, 100	12, 775	2. 54	158. 8	1-51	
18	...do	......do	....do		67, 600	16, 900	2. 60	162. 5	1-139	
19	...do	......do	....do		58, 600	14, 650	2. 54	158. 8	1-91	
20	Drab	Lime Island, Mich	....do		72, 000	18, 000	2. 50	156. 3	1-76	
21	...do	......do	....do		100, 000	25, 000	2. 58	161. 2	1-139	
22	...do	......do	....do		61, 700	15, 425	2. 551	159. 4	1-56	
23	...do	Marquette, Mich	On edge		32, 200	8, 050	2. 34	146. 3	1-23	Rather a clay stone.
24	...do	......do	On bed		31, 300	7, 825	2. 34	146. 3	1-23	
25	...do	......do	On edge		30, 400	7, 600	2. 34	46. 3	1-23	
26	Bluish-drab	Big Sturgeon Bay, Wis	On bed		86, 000	21, 500	2. 78	173. 8	1-399	A remarkably solid, stable stone.
27	...do	......do	On edge		66, 750	16, 687	2. 75	171. 9	1-678	
28	...do	Lemont Quarry, Cook County, Ill	On bed		48, 000	12, 000	2. 645	165. 3	1-89	
29	...do	......do	On edge		56, 000	14, 000	2. 645	165. 3	1-89	
30	Dark	Bardstown, Ky	On bed		65, 060	16, 250	2. 67	166. 9	1-80	Used for Louisville and Portland Canal.
31	...do	......do	On edge		60, 000	15, 000	2. 67	166. 9	1-80	Do.
32	White	Joliet, Ill	On bed		45, 000	11, 250	2. 55	159. 3	1-35	Specimens scant in measure, and not so good as Nos. 17 and 18 of same.
33	...do	......do	On edge		28, 200	7, 050	2. 55	159. 3	1-35	Do.
34	Dark-drab	Billingsville, Cooper County, Mo	On bed		26, 600	6, 650	2. 32	145.	1-23	
35	...do	......do	On edge		29, 000	7, 250	2. 32	145.	1-23	
36	Blue	Williamsville, Erie County, N. Y	On bed		49, 000	12, 250	2. 64	165.	0	
37	...do	......do	On edge		49, 500	12, 375	2. 64	165.	0	

* See Nos. 64, 65, and 66.

Crushing-strength of marbles in two-inch cubes.

Number.	Kind.	Locality.	Position.	Cracked.	Strength of specimen.	Strength per square inch.	Specific gravity.	Weight of one cubic foot.	Ratio of absorption.	Remarks.
				Pounds.	Pounds.	Pounds.		Pounds.		
1	East Chester	Tuckahoe, Westchester County, N. Y.	On bed		51, 800	12, 950	2. 875	179. 7	(*)	
2	do	do	do		48, 200	12, 050	2. 875	179. 7	(*)	
3	Common Italian	Italy	do		45, 000	11, 250	2. 690	168. 2	(*)	
4	do	do	do		52, 250	13, 062	2. 690	168. 2	(*)	
5	Vermont	Dorset, Bennington County, Vt	do		30, 450	7, 612	2. 635	164. 7	1-170	Crushed with slight explosion.
6	do	do	On edge		34, 680	8, 670	2. 683	167. 8	0	Do.
7	Drab	Mill Creek Quarry, Quincy, Ill	On bed		38, 750	9, 687	2. 570	160. 6	1-180	Crushed with louder explosion.
8	do	do	On edge		39, 150	9, 787	2. 510	156. 9	1-74	Do.
9	do	North Bay Quarry, Door County, Wis.	On bed		80, 100	20, 025	2. 800	175.	0	Crushed with quiet explosion.
10	do	do	On edge		54, 800	13, 700	2. 800	175.	0	Crushed with slight explosion; sand-cracks.

* The absorption of most appears so small, and occurs so slowly, that they were left for soakage hereafter.

Crushing-strength of sandstones in two-inch cubes.

Number.	Kind.	Locality.	Position.	Cracked.	Strength of specimen.	Strength per square inch.	Specific gravity.	Weight of one cubic foot.	Ratio of absorption.	Remarks.
1	Brown	Little Falls, N. Y	On bed		39, 400	9, 850	2. 250	140. 6	1-34	Used in building Trinity Church, New York City. Had been exposed for years to weather and become harder. Broke suddenly, without previous premonition.
2	do	do	On edge		36, 600	9, 150	2. 250	140. 6	1-34	
3	Gray	Bellville, N. J	On bed		46, 800	11, 700	2. 259	141.	1-27	Broke suddenly.
4	do	do	On edge		41, 000	10, 250	2. 259	141.	1-27	
5	Brown	Middletown, Conn	On bed		27, 800	6, 950	2. 360	148. 5	1-40	Trinity Church, Brooklyn, N. Y., built of it.
6	do	do	On edge		22, 200	5, 550	2. 360	148. 5	1-40	
7	Red	Haverstraw, N. Y	On bed		17, 400	4, 350	2. 130	133. 1	1-23	
8	do	do	On edge		16, 100	4, 025	2. 130	133. 1	1-23	
9	Pink	Medina, N. Y	On bed		69, 000	17, 250	2. 410	150. 6	1-55	Lilac in color.
10	do	do	On edge		59, 250	14, 812	2. 390	149. 3	1-51	More purple than last.
11	Drab	do	On bed		70, 900	17, 725	2. 420	151. 1	1-70	
12	do	Berea, Ohio	do		41, 000	10, 250	2. 110	131. 9	1-16	Very friable, like sugar.
13	do	do	do		33, 200	8, 300	2. 130	133. 1	1-20	
14	do	do	do		29, 000	7, 250	2. 200	137. 5	1-24	
15	do	do	do		31, 000	7, 750	2. 110	131. 9	1-19	
16	do	do	do		38, 400	9, 600	2. 140	133. 7	1-22	
17	Brownish-gray	North Amherst, Ohio	On edge		21, 800	5, 450	2. 140	133. 7	1-19	
18	do	do	On bed		26, 600	6, 650	2. 190	136. 9	1-19	
19	do	do	do		23, 100	5, 775	2. 160	135.	1-19	
20	Drab	Vermillion, Ohio	do		33, 800	8, 450	2. 160	135.	1-19	

21	....do	......do	....do	....	33, 000	8, 250	2. 165	135. 3	1-19	
22	....do	......do	....do	....	24, 000	6, 000	2. 165	135. 3	1-19	
23	....do	......do	....do	....	35, 400	8, 850	2. 157	134. 8	1-19	
24	....do	......do	....do	....	31, 400	7, 850	2. 157	134. 8	1-19	
25	....do	......do	On edge	....	27, 500	6, 875	2. 157	134. 8	1-19	
26	Purple	Fond du Lac, Wis	On bed	....	25, 000	6, 250	2. 220	138. 8	1-22	
27	....do	......do	....do	....	24, 900	6, 225	2. 220	138. 8	1-22	
28	....do	......do	On edge	....	20, 440	5, 110	2. 220	138. 8	1-22	
29	....do	Bass Island, Wis	On bed	....	21, 800	5, 450	2. 040	127. 5	1-15	
30	....do	......do	....do	....	17, 000	4, 250	2. 040	127. 5	1-15	
31	....do	......do	On edge	....	17, 150	4, 287	2. 040	127. 5	1-15	
32	....do	Marquette, Mich	On bed	....	20, 200	5, 050	2. 285	142. 8	1-32	
33	....do	......do	....do	....	29, 100	7, 275	2. 285	142. 8	1-32	
34	....do	......do	On edge	....	22, 600	5, 650	2. 285	142. 8	1-32	
35	....do	......do	On bed	....	29, 800	7, 450	2. 160	135.	1-20	
36	....do	......do	....do	....	29, 800	7, 450	2. 160	135.	1-20	
37	....do	......do	On edge	....	22, 920	5, 730	2. 160	135.	1-20	
38	....do	......do	On bed	....	21, 000	5, 250	2. 170	135. 6	1-20	
39	....do	......do	....do	....	25, 080	6, 270	2. 170	135. 6	1-20	
40	....do	......do	On edge	....	19, 000	4, 750	2. 170	135. 6	1-20	
41	Red-brown	Seneca freestone, Ohio	On bed	....	38, 750	9, 687	2. 390	149. 3	1-32	
42	....do	......do	On edge	....	42, 000	10, 500	2. 390	149. 3	1-32	
43	Olive-green	Cleveland, Ohio	On bed	....	27, 200	6, 800	2. 240	140.	1-37	
44	....do	......do	On edge	....	31, 640	7, 910	2. 240	140.	1-37	
45	Whitish	Marblehead, Ohio	On bed	....	31, 750	7, 937	2. 310	144. 4	1-19	Rather a chalky limestone.
46	....do	......do	On edge	....	27, 400	6, 850	2. 310	144. 4	1-19	Do.
47	Brown	Albion, Orleans County, N. Y	On bed	....	54, 000	13, 500	2. 420	151. 2	1-44	
48	....do	......do	On edge	....	45, 400	11, 350	2. 420	151. 2	1-44	
49	Pink	Kasota, Le Sueur County, Minn	On bed	27, 000	42, 800	10, 700	2. 630	164. 4	1-56	Calcareous sandstone.
50	....do	......do	On edge	....	46, 700	11, 675	2. 630	164. 4	1-56	
51	Light-buff	Fontenac, Goodhue County, Minn	On bed	....	25, 000	6, 250	2. 325	145. 3	1-28	
52	....do	......do	On edge	....	31, 100	7, 775	2. 325	145. 3	1-28	
53	Craigleith	Edinburgh, Scotland	On bed	....	48, 000	12, 000	2. 260	141. 3	1-34	
54	....do	......do	On edge	....	45, 000	11, 250	2. 260	141. 3	1-34	
55	Freestone	Dorchester, New Brunswick	On bed	....	36, 600	9, 150	....	....	....	
56	....do	......do	....do	....	37, 650	9, 412	....	....	....	
57	Olive	......do	....do	....	17, 000	4, 250	....	....	....	
58	....do	......do	On edge	....	24, 200	6, 050	....	....	....	

O

www.ingramcontent.com/pod-product-compliance
Lightning Source LLC
LaVergne TN
LVHW020643110826
845149LV00004B/1326

* 9 7 8 1 4 1 8 1 9 0 3 9 2 *